MARRIAGE

21 YEARS OF DOING IT WRONG, 21 DAYS TO MAKE IT RIGHT

WINSTON TYRONE JACKSON, SR.

Rain Publishing

KNIGHTDALE, NORTH CAROLINA

Copyright © 2014 by **Winston T. Jackson, Sr.**

All rights reserved. No part of this publication may be reproduced, distributed or transmitted in any form or by any means, including photo-copying, recording, or other electronic or mechanical methods, without the prior written permission of the publisher, except in the case of brief quotations embodied in critical reviews and certain other noncommercial uses permitted by copyright law. For permission requests, write to the publisher, addressed "Attention: Permissions Coordinator," at the address below.

Winston T. Jackson, Sr.
Address: P.O. Box 442343, Jacksonville, FL. 32222
Email: winstontjackson@yahoo.com
Twitter: @winston_jackson
Facebook: www.facebook.com/winstontjacksonsr
Website: www.WinstonTJacksonSr.com

Edited by Rain Publishing/www.RainPublishing.com
Cover Photography: Lenara Funk Photography/www.lenarafunk.com
Cover Design: Trevis C. Bailey/www.SDCreativeWorks.com

Ordering Information:
Quantity sales. Special discounts are available on quantity purchases by corporations, associations, and others. For details, contact the "Special Sales Department" at the address above.

Marriage – 21 Years of Doing it Wrong, 21 Days to Make it Right/ Winston T. Jackson, Sr. – 2nd ed.
ISBN 978-0-9899742-9-5
Library of Congress Control Number: 2014936240

About the Book

Many marriages perish because of a lack of understanding. They do not have God's foundational principles or the knowledge of His plan for marriage. Therefore, they live unhappy, unfulfilled and miserable for as many as fifty years. This book will identify the many failure points that can lead to an unhealthy marriage or worse, divorce. It was these failure points that ultimately lead to my divorce after 21 years of marriage. Now, God has revealed to me the recipe for living a prosperous, joy-filled and healthy marriage which I will share with you.

The key is to "Renew Your Mind to God's Design." This book will empower you with 21 ways to do marriage right. These are 21 simple, yet not so easy steps that, if done correctly, will lead you into a marriage that is blessed by God. Marriage is not easy, but once you understand and apply the principles, you will find it becomes easier and more fulfilling.

While reading this book you will find yourself thinking, "How will these principles apply to my spouse?" However, if you are the one who is reading it, then it applies directly to you. You will get a renewed and fresh approach on how you respond to your spouse. This will be the beginning of a healthy marriage relationship. Also, as you read through this book, open up your Bible, read and meditate on the Scriptures referenced. God will enlighten your understanding of what His Word is and to His design and purpose for marriage.

My Prayer

Father God, in the name of Jesus, I thank You for the opportunity to write this book. I humble myself before You and I pray that it brings glory to Your name. This book was not written for my glory, but for Yours, not for my fame, but for the edification of Your people. I pray that every person reading this book will have their understanding increased. Let them see wondrous things in Your Word. Let the spirit of wisdom, knowledge and understanding flow freely. Let them see clearly Your divine plan for their marriage and the sanctity of their union. I declare that each person reading this book is protected against any and all devices of the enemy. I declare boldly that Satan and his angels are defeated as I embark on the mission of Killing the Demon of Divorce. In every church, in every home, in every workplace, in every country, on every continent, all across this world, divorce is defeated! Father I lift up every child: children of divorced families, children from healthy marriages and children in single-parent homes. Let them grow into adulthood having no understanding of divorce. Let them know of only one way, that is Your way, Your plan! Let Your Word of life reign true and mighty upon this earth. It's in the mighty name of Jesus that I pray, Amen.

This book is dedicated to my lovely wife, Cathy Michele Jackson. God promised me years ago that He would give me the wife He needed me to have and that wife is you. You are my best friend, my coach, my spiritual advisor and my lover. I love you very much!

Special Acknowledgement

Gerald Griffin, LtCol. USMC (Retired)

When I met you over 27 years ago, you were doing what you do best, encouraging, motivating and empowering others to be the best possible person they could be. Who would have known that through the many years of being thousands of miles apart, you would still be doing the same thing for me? Thanks for not just inspiring me, motivating me, encouraging me and for always being there for me, but for believing in me.

Special Thanks

I would like to express a special thank you to the most dynamic Pastors on the planet, Pastors Michael and Connie Smith of The Church of Jacksonville. It is because of your God-ordained ministry and leadership that my life has changed for the better. "Happy is the man who finds wisdom, and the man who gains understanding Proverbs 3:13" (NKJV). I found wisdom and happiness under your leadership. Thank you! May God continue to bless you! I love you guys!

Acknowledgements

My Mother – Mamie Jackson
Special Sister – Sandra Jackson

Thanks for taking care of me in my time of need. You not only prayed for me, but you fed me, and catered to my every need. I love you both!!!

My Sons –
Winston T. Jackson, II
Travis L. Jackson
My Grandson -
Winston T. Jackson, III

Let's create a legacy of Jackson men who fear the Lord. Let us become a generation who honors, respects, and loves their wives "even as" Christ also loved the church. Let's change a generation so that your children's children will call you blessed. I love you guys!!!

My Siblings – Curtis, Jean, Linda, Royce, Patricia and Cynthia

Thanks for being there for me at my lowest time in life. I pray that the seeds you have sown into my life will be greatly multiplied.

Special Friend and Sister in Christ – Diane Grant
Thanks for your encouragement, prayers and for your belief in me. Thanks for being a follower of God and being led by the Spirit…you know what I mean.

Life Long Friends –
Anthony "Tony Hamp" Hamilton
Noah C. Battle, Sr.
El Jerome Battle
Kenneth C. Truett (R.I.P.)
Frank Murphy

My brothers from other mothers. We have been together for many, many years and I thank God for friends like you, friends who endure through good and bad times. Love you guys!!!

CONTENTS

Sow the Seed of Realizing God's Love for You 1

Sow the Seed of Learning to Love You 3

Sow the Seed of Committing to Change YOU 7

Sow the Seed of Controlling Your Thought Life 11

Sow the Seed of Self-Examination: You vs. Scripture 15

Sow the Seed of Making Your Spouse Most Important 17

Sow the Seed of Making Daily Investments 21

Sow the Seed of Praying for and with Your Spouse DAILY 23

Sow the Seed of Asking God to Teach You How to Love Your Mate 27

Sow the Seed of Planning Activities for You and Your Mate 29

Sow the Seed of Living and Loving in the Spirit 31

Sow the Seed of Examining the Impact of Current Friends and Family 35

Sow the Seed of Constantly Discovering 39

Sow the Seed of Learning the Essence of Forgiveness 43

Sow the Seed of Speaking Words of Empowerment and Encouragement 47

Sow the Seed of Understanding Marriage is TWO Individuals Trying to Live as One 51

Sow the Seed of Racing to Embrace and Say I Love You, Face to Face 55

Sow the Seed of Being a Partner and a Friend 59

Sow the Seed of Understanding, Everybody Plays the Fool Sometimes! 63
Sow the Seed of Practicing Honesty Even if it Hurts 67
Sow the Seed of Knowing Right vs. Righteous 71
You Did It! 75
My Husband – My Shepherd 77
Book Order Form 87

FOREWORD

What can be said about a book that has been truly inspired by the Word of God? Thoughts from the mind of The Father are apparent from the very first word of this manuscript straight through to the very last word. There are hundreds, perhaps thousands of books, articles and papers all over this world that can provide possible solutions to struggling married couples. So, what makes this book different? This book demonstrates that God is not finished with the salvation of marriages, yet. Since the beginning of time, God's focus has always been on godly marital relationships that would last forever.

Marriage is the covenant relationship instituted by God, Himself. He started this relationship process with Adam and Eve in the Garden of Eden. Since God is totally sold on relationships, He has not given up on those who have failed to keep their marriage vows. He has, however, opened up the windows of heaven and revealed one more God-ordained thought to yet another willing servant, who will share the revelation in this text.

Mr. Winston Tyrone Jackson made a decision to obey God. As a first time author, Mr. Jackson has very nicely put this revelation in a book. Mr. Jackson's book has been written with much anticipation, joy and excitement. First, it is simply written; it is very clear and understandable; and it is pleasant to read. The principles are "do-able." Application and practice for the desired lifestyle changes are realistic and attainable.

The best of the best of this book is that Mr. Jackson has been ordained by God to write this phenomenal message to people regardless of who they are or their standard of living. The significance of this message can benefit men or women, singles or married, divorcees or widowed; old adults, young adults or teens; religious or nonreligious, rich or poor, highly educated or educated, the indifferent and all others. Anyone can digest what has been shared in this brilliant writing.

Writing a book of this magnitude in such a way that any person can gain from it has to be attributed to Mr. Jackson's love for God. His love for God can be proven by his obedience to God to write this book. This book could give guidance to the development, growth and management of the most important institution on earth, the institution of MARRIAGE. His submission and respect for Who God Is has brought some powerful answers to some pretty hardcore issues into the open, which confront a countless number of couples worldwide every day.

The toughest charge of this assignment for Mr. Jackson was to allow God to help him put his personal story before the entire world in this book. He literally had to put his faith on the line and release himself; then, he looked into the mirror at how he played the game in his marriage; and now he is giving the rest of us a peek.

My journey with Mr. Jackson through the process of writing his book has been a wonderful experience. It has been my pleasure and a delightful honor to be a part of something I believe will cause innumerable marriages and families to change and turn toward a more godly direction. I highly recommend the reading of this book to those who are not married, as this is an excellent opportunity to learn how to build a solid foundation in their own hearts and minds concerning all covenant relationships.

Much success to Tyrone and Cathy,

Cynthia Franklin Anderson, PH. D.

A Word of Encouragement

Serving in the Marine Corps for over 31 years, I had the privilege and opportunity to serve alongside Winston Jackson nearly 27 years ago. Our friendship never faded and even though he left the Marine Corps after achieving the rank of Sergeant, I continued service through the enlisted and warrant officer ranks and finally retired as a Lieutenant Colonel. Winston and I never lost contact through the many years.

Winston desired a marriage that would last forever; however, we learn through life that it doesn't go the way we plan. Therefore, building your marriage on a solid foundation is essential.

This book provides a good road map to encourage you in planting a good seed so that the harvest will not only be rewarding to you and your spouse but will bring glory to God. This builds that foundation for a healthier and happy marriage. Through this book, Winston will assist you in building a solid foundation. The 21 steps outlined may sound simple; however, it is a work in progress that if followed from the heart continuously will produce a fairytale marriage in the real world.

Gerry J. Griffin
Lieutenant Colonel, United States Marine Corps (Retired)

The Cover

The ring on the cover was worn for 21 years and had to be involuntarily cut off my finger following a motorcy-cle accident. The ring symbolizes the brokenness that resulted from living in marriage wrongly for so many years. What once represented a future of never-ending togetherness and a growing old and gray together, now represented the beginning of the end.

The shattered watch on the cover was damaged during the same motorcycle accident. It stopped at 2:17 pm on that October day, forever marking the exact time my life was shattered (or so I thought). More importantly, it represents the time God began rebuilding me. Although there were many sleepless nights, tears on my pillow and pain in my heart, God changed me forever! I am so grateful to Him!

Winston T. Jackson, Sr.

Preface

How I did it Wrong for 21 Years

Here is a very real and true picture of how I did marriage wrong for 21 years. The purpose of this book is to be transparent and to stop hiding behind shame, pride, guilt and ignorance. Many marriages end in divorce. The couple simply did not understand God's purpose and design for marriage. Too many couples are too proud to discuss or disclose the full truth about what has caused the breakdown of their marriage. If we could eliminate our pride, open up and share our lessons learned with others, we would have fewer divorces.

My marriage did not begin on a firm foundation. Early on there were unaddressed "concerns" that caused offenses that were never resolved. As a married man, now armed with an offense that was growing larger, I felt the need to be liked and to be attractive to the opposite sex even more than before. Anytime a woman would praise me, tell me I looked nice and that I dressed nice, or how they were impressed with my intellect, they drew me closer to them. Little did I know this was simply a strategy of the enemy planting seeds of doubt and distrust that led to division and insecurity.

I knew that having extramarital affairs was wrong. I knew what I was doing could be the downfall of my marriage…I just did not know how to fix it. Eventually I would stop, by choice, because I always wanted to live a godly life and I always wanted to have my family active in the church. For years I was faithful: teaching Sunday school, spending time with my sons and involved in healthy extracurricular activities; life was good. Still, something was missing from my marriage. It was still incomplete, still broken.

I was dissatisfied with how things were. Once again, along came the seductress, quietly sneaking in to pacify me. My sexual and nonsexual needs were not being met at home. In fact, I did not even know what my needs were. I thought I was a pervert (that is what she jokingly called me from time to time). I did not feel like "the man" in my own house and I did not know how to get my needs met through my wife. I got caught up in "this is the way it is" and never pursued a genuine understanding from using the Word of God, nor did I seek direction from my elders or spiritual leaders. I heard to tithe and to trust in God. I was taught the 23rd Psalm and the Ten Commandments. I do not know how many times I was taught "He died, I said He died, but early one Sunday morning, He got up!" Of the many pastors and thousands of sermons I have heard, not one of them taught me how to be a husband.

My "Ah hah!" Moment

As I begin to seek the wisdom of God, I stood at my stove with the Bible in my hand and the stove light beaming down upon it. My prayer was for God to direct me to a passage that He wanted me to see. As I flipped the Book open, it fell miraculously upon Ephesians, chapter five. As I began to read, it was as if a spotlight pointed to one place on the page and that was verse 25. The most intense light illuminated the words, "Present her to Himself a glorious church." It was in these seven words that my journey of understanding began. It was here I decided I wanted the same type of gift Christ was preparing to give to Himself, "A glorious church, without spot or wrinkle."

So How Do I Get This Glorious Wife?

In order for me to get this understanding, I had to establish this truth… my marriage relationship should be a direct reflection of the relationship Christ has with the church. Christ is the husband and the "church" is His wife. As I looked at the interaction Jesus had with His people (the church), I saw a living, breathing, realistic model for how I was to interact with my wife. Although that marriage ended, it was in the misfortune of my divorce that your blessing will come. Satan took advantage of my first marriage. Through that experience God promises to save many marriages, including yours, if you commit to allowing Him.

Introduction

God designed the world to function solely on this one principle: Plant a seed and it will produce a harvest. This principle was first introduced during the creation of the world and can be found in Genesis 1:11-12 (NIV), "Then God said, "Let the land produce vegetation: seed-bearing plants and trees on the land that bear fruit with seed in it, according to their various kinds." And it was so. The land produced vegetation: plants bearing seed according to their kinds and trees bearing fruit with seed in it according to their kinds. And God saw that it was good. God created the foundation (the land), and that land would produce vegetation. The vegetation would then produce a seed that would bear fruit. This principle is perpetual in its action and purpose. In this book, you will see just how important this principle of "planting a seed and producing a harvest" is to your everyday life and in your marriage. Many of us have heard the phrase, "You reap what you sow," which originated from this principle of planting and producing a harvest.

It is important to get an understanding of the two definitions below before applying this book to your marriage:

Seed – The element used to produce, increase and reproduce in its likeness. It's the initial investment used in expectation of an increased return.

Fruit/Harvest - Anything produced or accruing; product, result, or effect; return or profit: the fruits of one's labors. It is the harvest from the initial seed planted. In the financial world this is called ROI or Return on Investment.

God created us and commanded us to "be fruitful" Genesis 1:28 (NIV). Until sin entered into the world, this action of being fruitful was always good. If you planted the seed of a good deed, then you would reap the harvest of a good deed. Anything you gave or did for someone else would be multiplied and returned to you. Once sin entered into the world the principle remained true; however, a new type of seed was introduced, one that produces bad fruit.

Therefore, understanding the concept of seed and fruit will help you to follow the concept of this book. It is designed to get you planting seeds of true love the way God planned it. Once seeds of true love are planted, you will have no choice except to receive the multiplied fruit of true love in return.

In this book there are 21 Seeds of Love that must be planted in order to reap the fruit of a good marriage relationship. There are also 21 Affirmations and 21 Prayers for each seed. You must verbally confess them daily. Unlike most devotional books that give you something for each day, these seeds build day upon day. After you have planted your 21st seed, start again with the first seed and continue planting the seeds, confessing the affirmations and most of all, praying about your need and cultivating that seed. You should refuse to put this book down until this process of sowing seeds becomes a part of your everyday life. You will surely reap the harvest of a love-filled marriage, one that is truly blessed by God!

Remember, as long as you continue to plant good seed, you will continue to reap a good harvest. However, there are two things that can stop this process: 1) when you cease to plant seed, you cease to produce a harvest and 2) planting a counteractive seed. If you are planting good seed and bad seed at the same time, you will kill the process, break the cycle and never produce good fruit.

You will notice that each of the Affirmations begins with "Today, I commit..." This is because commitments cannot be changed, modified, adjusted or cancelled. When you read the Affirmations, read them as a verbal confession of your commitment to God, your spouse and yourself. There is also a Prayer for each seed sown. The Affirmations and Prayers should always be spoken aloud, not read silently. Also remember that sowing a seed is an action; therefore, the 21 Seeds are not just for reading, they are for application. You must DO them; take action.

Day One

Sow the Seed of... Realizing God's Love for You

The first and most important element towards creating a spirit-filled marriage resides in this understanding: God Loves You! Plant this seed in your heart, water it and nourish it daily by praying, reading and applying His Word. From this very moment in time to the second you breathe your last breath, understanding God's love for you is the seed you need in order to begin loving your spouse and seeing the fruit of a God-blessed marriage. Knowing God loves you means that you can trust in His Word, His leadings and in the Holy Spirit.

Here's the good news: God desires you to have a great marriage! If you are separated, in divorce court, divorced, in an "okay" marriage, or already in a great marriage, God wants to give you more. His Word says in Ephesians 3:20 (NKJV), "Now to Him who is able to do exceedingly abundantly above all that we ask or think, according to the power that works in us." The key to receiving the exceedingly, abundantly and above is having "the power working in us." You obtain and increase this power by your knowledge of and obedience to the Word of God. Now the words "exceedingly," "abundantly," and "above," are Paul's way of saying God's giving is an unceasing increase that has no end. So regardless of where you are in your marriage life, God's desire is to give you a better marriage and then, improve upon that; then improve upon the improvement and so on and so on...He loves you just that much!!! Continue to sow the seed of God's love for you and watch as you reap a harvest of love multiplied again and again.

Affirmation

Today, I commit to receiving all of the love that God has for me. I know and understand that He and He alone is my source of life, joy, peace, patience, and most of all, love. Regardless of my current marital status, I KNOW that God is willing to meet my needs and then continue to exceed them.

Prayer

Father, I thank You for Your love. Thank You for loving me so much that You gave Your only Son, Jesus. I believe in Him, I rely on Him and therefore receive Your gift of a good life filled with Your blessings of love, joy and peace. Romans 8:37-39 states that nothing (no thing) can separate Your love from me. Forgive me, O Lord, for the times when I am weak; I trust in You to restore me, cleanse me and make me pure in Your sight. Whatever I ask You for, according to John 14:14, You will do it. Thank You for far more than I could ever imagine. It is in Jesus' name I pray, Amen.

Day Two

Sow the Seed of... Learning to Love You

One key to a successful marriage is learning to love you. Many people seek an external source to find love for themselves. They believe if they love others, they will receive love in return. That is somewhat true; however, the foundation for loving someone else is first built on knowing God loves you, then second, learning to love yourself. You must first possess love in order to give love. God gives love to you; you receive that love for yourself and then give to love others.

When Jesus says in Matthew 19:19 that we should love our neighbors as ourselves, the qualifier to loving your neighbor is having a love for yourself. In Ephesians 5:28 (NKJV), Paul speaks to husbands along this same line when he says, "Husbands ought to love their wives as their own body; he, who loves his wife, loves himself." Again, the qualifier is to love you.

You will learn to appreciate the beauty of God that He placed in you by way of the Holy Spirit. When God breathed the breath of life in you, you were made complete with ALL of the fruit of the Spirit in you. Galatians 5:22 (NKJV) says, *"The fruit of the Spirit is love, joy, peace, longsuffering, kindness, goodness, faithfulness, gentleness and self-control."* Although some may find this hard to believe, He's in you; that's who you are! Let me put it another way. God placed a seed in you (The Holy Spirit) and the harvest from that seed is the fruit of the Spirit. So not only do you have love in you, you are love. No external force can tap into that love other than you; once you get it, you can freely give it unconditionally and never-ending.

This seed of loving yourself is one that mass produces internally, yet its fruit is displayed externally. A person who loves himself/herself is confident and self-reliant, not dependent upon someone else's love to feel good about him/her. This person of self-worth and self-confidence is very attractive, especially to your spouse.

Affirmation

Today I commit to a full investigation of the love of God placed in me. I will seek God for the Holy Spirit to reveal and increase my understanding of what a precious gift of love I am to God and to myself. I will look beyond those things the world sees as attractive and only seek to please the Father and myself, therefore pleasing my spouse.

Prayer

Father, I realize that before I can love others, I must first love myself. I am created in Your image and likeness; therefore, I am fearfully and wonderfully made, according to Psalm 139:14. I submit my thought life to come into agreement with Your thoughts concerning me. I thank You Lord for loving me, even more than I love myself. Your love is shed abroad in my heart and I will love others just as I love myself. As a husband, I look to Christ as my example of how to love my wife. As a wife, I submit to my husband as is fitting to the Lord. I give You all honor, glory and praise, in Jesus' name, Amen.

Day Three

Sow the Seed of... Committing to Change YOU

Most couples enter into a relationship because there are so many positive things they like about each other. However, as they really get to know each other they begin to notice "character flaws." They either decide they can deal with them or think the other partner will change. What they really mean is, "I can change that!" This is one of the biggest mistakes we make in relationships. You cannot change the things you consider as flaws in another person. Only God and the person can change themselves. What you can do is change the way <u>you</u> respond to those imperfect behaviors!

The only person you truly have control over is yourself. Therefore, if you commit to change your response to the things you do not like, you will find more peace and tranquility in your marriage. There is nothing wrong with letting your spouse know you do not like certain behaviors or disagree with something said or done. If you discover that it is who they are, do not let their actions impact you, your actions or your emotions.

Even if what they are doing is ungodly, your response and reaction should always be godly. A godly response is one that promotes righteousness and peace. Be willing to love your partner enough to adjust to them. When both parties are making adjustments, you are bound to get the perfect fit.

As the Bible says in 1 Corinthians 13:7 (NKJV), Love *"endures all things."* In order to reflect the true love of God, we must endure the things we do not necessarily like or agree with. The word "endure" means to remain firm under suffering or misfortune. We may have to endure something for a very long time. If you are going to deal with it, you may as well make the best of it.

To help you with planting the seed of changing yourself, refer to a familiar passage of Scripture found in Romans 12:2 renewing your mind to the things of God. You want to think with the mind of Christ, which is one of humility, esteeming others higher than yourselves, becoming a servant and putting aside your desires and your aspirations for those of others. In this and all seeds, look to God for your harvest. He is faithful to reward you greatly.

Affirmation

Today, I commit to changing ME and not my spouse. I realize that it is within my control to react or not. The way I handle my dislikes is my choice, so I choose to respond in a way that promotes peace and brings glory to God. I am in control of my emotions, actions and reactions. No one can make me angry, nor make me unhappy unless I give them permission to do so.

Prayer

Father, in the name of Jesus, renew my mind to the things of God that I might prove what is Your acceptable and perfect will for my life. Let nothing I do be done through selfish ambition or conceit, but in lowliness of mind, esteeming others better than myself. Make me like-minded with Christ that I might endure all things in lowliness and meekness of heart, serving others as I serve You in Jesus' name, Amen.

Day Four

Sow the Seed of...
Controlling Your Thought Life

"Finally, brethren, whatever things are true, whatever things are noble, whatever things are just, whatever things are pure, whatever things are lovely, whatever things are of good report, if there is any virtue and if there is anything praiseworthy - <u>meditate on these things.</u> The things which you learned and received and heard and saw in me, these do, and the God of peace will be with you." Philippians 4:8-9 (NKJV).

"I wonder who she is with." "Why did he say that?" "I know she likes him." "Look at her, smiling in his face." "He is not answering the phone because he does not want me to know where he is." ALL of this thinking is out-of-control thinking and it will destroy your marriage. Even if your thoughts are valid, if they are rooted in fear, they are of the devil! God desires for you to live in peace, yes even in the midst of a storm. The Bible says, "Cast your burden on the LORD, And He shall sustain you; He shall never permit the righteous to be moved" Psalm 55:22 (NKJV).

Know this: You are in control of what goes on in your mind. Poor thoughts can lead to poor choices, which can lead to poor actions, which can lead to destructive behavior. Destructive behavior can lead to divorce, jail and even worse, death.

Affirmation

Today, I commit to replacing ALL thoughts that do not line up with the Word of God. Should any thought of fear, anxiety or selfishness attempt to enter and control my mind, I vow to replace those thoughts by meditating on whatever things are true, noble, just, pure, lovely and of a good report (Philippians 4:8).

Prayer

Father, I thank You for Your Word, for it brings life to my very bones. Forgive me, O Lord, for allowing even my thoughts to not line up with Your Word. I desire only to meditate and to think about things that are just, pure, lovely, noble, of good report, virtuous and praiseworthy. I cast all of my cares upon You and depend on You to sustain me. Although I walk in the flesh, I do not war according to the flesh. For the weapons of my warfare are not carnal but mighty in God for pulling down strongholds. I decree 2 Corinthians 10:5 and cast down arguments and every high thing that exalts itself against the knowledge of God, bringing every thought into captivity to the obedience of Christ. I submit my thoughts unto You and I guard them diligently, knowing that they affect everything I do. I bless, praise and glorify Your name, in Jesus' name, Amen.

Day Five

Sow the Seed of... Self-Examination: You vs. Scripture

In Ephesians 5:22-25 NKJV, you will notice that the Word never gives a command to the couple but to the individual that makes up the couple. To the wife, it says, *"Submit to your husband as to the Lord,"* and to the husband it says, *"Love your wives, just as Christ also loved the church and gave Himself for her."* You don't see God's commandment to the wife saying, "Your husband is to love you as Christ also loved the church." The intention is for you to do what is commanded of you, not looking at what the other party has to do or is failing to do.

Sow the seed of a daily Self-Examination to see if you are in line with the way God instructed **you** to love. If **you** are failing in any area, make a commitment to fix **you** and let God do the work on your spouse. This takes a great deal of trust in God, but Who better to trust with your marriage and spouse than the One who created you both.

Take a close look at 1 Corinthians 13: 1-8 (NKJV). Do you love with humility, placing the needs of your spouse ahead of yours? Are you patient, longsuffering and kind? Are you truthful with your spouse? Have your actions been rude, provoking or self-gratifying? If you find any areas where YOU are lacking, pray and seek God's counsel on how to fix them. This seed of self-examination will help you see yourself. It will produce the fruit of a better you who is easier to give love and easier to receive love. Remember, this cycle of sowing and reaping never ends, it only gets better.

Affirmation

Today, I commit to a daily Self-Examination of my contributions to the health of my marriage. Anything that I find that does not agree with God's plan, I vow to remove it. Then, I will ask God for wisdom and understanding on how to be a better wife/husband for my spouse. I know He will answer and give it to me liberally.

Prayer

Father, I thank You for Your Word, for your Word is alive in me; therefore, I call it forth to illuminate my areas of weakness. I commit to meditate on Luke 6:41-42 and examine myself daily. Forgive, sanctify and cleanse me, O Lord, according to Ephesians 5:26 that I might be Holy by the washing of water by the Word. The Spirit of the Lord is within me; therefore I have knowledge, wisdom and understanding of Your Word. I receive Your instructions and submit to Your way. Thank You for hearing and granting this prayer, in Jesus' name, Amen.

Day Six

Sow the Seed of... Making Your Spouse Most Important

I might say this seed is THE MOST VALUABLE seed you can sow. If not the most valuable, it is certainly in the top three. This seed will probably produce a harvest faster than any other seed. Why? It's simple. We were all created with some basic needs: the need to love and to be loved, to be cared for, to be heard and to feel like we matter to someone. What makes it produce a harvest so quickly? When it is planted, it is actually being planted in both you and your spouse. It grows in two separate places; yet, it grows together. In you, it meets the need of loving someone and that activates compassion within you and makes you want to love more. In your spouse, it meets the need of knowing that he/she matters to you, that they are heard, cared for and loved.

Besides your relationship with God, nothing or no one else comes ahead of your spouse. Learn to put the urgent, important and the traditional in their proper perspectives. Put away the laptop, get off the telephone, turn the television off and give your undivided attention to your spouse. You may be a master at multi-tasking; however, you cannot give 100% attention to your spouse while doing *anything* else. Church, work, children, finances, parents, and friends all take a back seat to your marriage. Remember, we were made in the image and likeness of God and this characteristic is the same as one of the Ten Commandments, "*You shall have no other gods before me*" Deuteronomy 5:7 (NKJV). When you place a person, activity or thing ahead of your relationship with your spouse, the message you are ultimately sending is "that thing/person is more important than he/she is." This can do great damage to your marriage.

Spending dedicated time with your spouse should be done with the same level of intense attention as you have when watching the game of the week or that favorite talk show. LISTEN!!! Know what's going on with your spouse. Be able to provide a play-by-play of what they are saying and follow-up with them from time to time on that particular subject. This lets your spouse KNOW that you are interested in him/her. This seed will produce and reproduce faster than you can keep up.

Affirmation

Today, I commit to focusing on the needs of my spouse. Whatever things or people might be preventing me from showing my spouse that he/she is the single most important thing to me next to my relationship with God, I vow to eliminate or re-prioritize. I will depend upon the Holy Spirit to guide and teach me. I will depend on the Holy Spirit to lead me to a healthy, happy and God-ordained marriage.

Prayer

Father, I thank You for this Man/Woman of God that You have placed in my life. I pray for Your forgiveness in any area where I may have failed to please You or to please her/him. I submit myself to her/him out of reverence to Christ, recognizing Christ as the head of our lives. I look to You as my Source for meeting my needs and I rely on the Holy Spirit to reveal to me Your way to meet the needs of my spouse. According to Daniel 2:22, reveal to me the deep and secret things, for You know what is in the darkness, in Jesus' name, Amen.

Day Seven

Sow the Seed of...
Making Daily Investments

A strong and healthy marriage requires daily investments that will provide daily returns. Remember this: yesterday's deposit is history.

Make daily deposits such as:
Let me rub your back for you tonight.
I'll give the kids a bath; you chill.
I'll clean up the kitchen; you do nothing.
Email/text/write a short poem of appreciation.
Shut-up and listen... just listen, really listen!
Let your spouse know you are proud of him/her.

Remember, love is not a feeling or an emotion. Feelings and emotions are the result of love being expressed, not love itself. There are countless things you can do for your spouse to show your love. It does not have to cost you a cent, just a commitment. Love is something you do; so do something DAILY!

Affirmation

Today, I commit to making daily deposits that will strengthen my marriage. I know and understand that in order for my marriage to improve, it is up to me! I purpose to study what things make my spouse happy and comfortable then do them consistently. I do not look to her/him for the return on my investment, I look to God.

Prayer

Father, I thank You for Your love towards me. Forgive me, O Lord, for my selfish and self-centered thoughts and actions. I humble myself before You and I seek Your direction in pleasing my spouse. I pray Philippians 2:3, that nothing I do be done selfishly or in conceitedness but in lowliness of mind, esteeming others more than myself. Help me Father to sow seeds of goodness into my wife/husband and I look to You, not her/him for a fruitful harvest. I know that if I obey You, I will remain in Your love and Your joy will overflow in my life. I want to love my spouse in that same way, giving my life to serve as I serve You, in Jesus' name, Amen.

Day Eight

Sow the Seed of... Praying for and with Your Spouse DAILY

Prayer is a time of fellowship and worshipping with the Father. It should always begin with praise and thanksgiving, then asking for forgiveness, provision, and protection against evil. Since God knows us and knows what is best for our lives, we pray that His Will be done in our lives; then, we end the prayer with honoring and acknowledging who He is in our lives. We then close the prayer with thanksgiving.

When praying for your spouse, the same format applies; however, your requests become more personal. Pray and even lay hands on your spouse as you pray, interceding on their behalf. Thank God for your spouse, pray for their provision and protection from illness and danger, that no hurt or harm comes near her/him. Pray for her/him to receive God's wisdom, for her/his prosperity and that God would give her/him the desires of his/her heart. Also, make your prayer specific by addressing such needs as favor at a job interview and problems she/he may be having at work. Pray that God will open his/her heart to receive all that He has for her/him.

You must spend time alone in prayer and also spend time in prayer with your spouse daily. If your spouse is unwilling to participate, then pray for your spouse during your alone time with God. Pray as though she/he was present, using words like "we" and "us." Intercede on her/his behalf.

God desires us to rely on Him daily to seek His guidance, His provision and His protection. He wants us in constant communication with Him, sensitive to His voice and obedient to His Word. Jesus said in Luke 18:1 (NKJV) "... *that men always ought to pray and not lose heart.*" Consistently communicate with God, making known your need of Him, then never give up. Every opportunity you get, you should be praying. Even if it is for just five seconds walking down the aisle at the grocery store, pray.

Why does God want us praying to Him daily? The answer is found in Deuteronomy 8:3 (NLT) - to teach us that people need more than bread for their lives; real life comes by feeding on every Word of the LORD.

Praying for your spouse is one of the most valuable seeds that can be sown. Why? It says to the Father, I honor You, I need You and I trust You with my life and the life of my spouse. God honors that because it is His desire for your life; it is His Word. It also communicates to your spouse that you love them so much that you are willing to seek God on her/his behalf daily. Not for your personal benefit, but for her/him.

God honors that and will answer your prayers. 1 John 5:14-15 (NKJV) reveals this: *"Now this is the confidence that we have in Him that if we ask anything according to His will, He hears us. And if we know that He hears us, whatever we ask, we know that we have the petitions that we have asked of Him."* That's great news! Look at the qualifiers for getting your prayers answered: 1) we must ask and 2) the request must be according to His will. So you say, "the asking is easy but how do I know what is His will?" That is just as simple. His Will is written in His Word. So, yep… you need to know His Word in order to know His Will. His Will is to bless you; and to find out how He desires to bless you, study Deuteronomy 8:7-20.

Remember this: your prayer time is a time of dialogue between you and God. Be prepared to speak as well as listen.

Affirmation

Today, I commit to establishing/increasing my prayer life. I commit to seeking the Father daily on behalf of my spouse and my family. I believe God wants me to have a blessed life and a blessed marriage, therefore, I seek Him daily for His direction and instructions for my life.

Prayer

Father in the name of Jesus, I come into Your presence thanking You for my life, for my spouse and my children. Forgive me dear God for not seeking Your face daily and not depending on You. Father I desire a closer walk with You. You said in James 4:8 as I draw close to You, You would draw close to me; therefore, I believe You walk and talk with me throughout every day. I depend on You for my provision, so give me this day my daily bread. Father protect me from the evil one and his plans to destroy my family and me. Lead me, O Lord, into the land of prosperity; order my every step; and invade my thoughts with thoughts of good and not evil. I submit my will to You that Your Will is done in my life this day. I thank You that You hear and answer my prayer, in Jesus' name, Amen.

Day Nine

Sow the Seed of... Asking God to Teach You How to Love Your Mate

Many of us are clueless when it comes to knowing how to love our spouses. God desires for you to have a deeper level of intimacy, one that is custom-made for you and your spouse. Since He is the one who created your spouse, He knows more about what it takes to please him/her than he/she knows himself/herself.

Upon creation we took on the image and likeness of God. When God made man and woman, each of them took on 100% of the image and likeness of God. Therefore, God knows who needs what to be satisfied. Furthermore, He can drill down into the individual's personality and the world that shaped his/her ways and give you specific tailor-made instructions on how to please him/her.

"But the Helper, the Holy Spirit, whom the Father will send in My name, He will teach you all things, and bring

to your remembrance all things that I said to you" John 14:26 (NKJV).

Depend on the Holy Spirit, whom God sent, to teach you all things and to help you to remember the things that He has already taught you. By following this spiritual guide, you are destined for success and happiness in your marriage.

Affirmation

Today, I commit to personal time in prayer, asking God to continue to teach me how to love my spouse. I believe God's Word when it says the Holy Spirit will guide me into all truths and will teach me all things. I surrender my own leanings and understandings and submit to the Holy Spirit for direction.

Prayer

Father, I thank You for creating me in Your image and Your likeness. Forgive me Father for the thoughts, acts and deeds that were not pleasing in Your sight. Lord, I recognize You as my source for life; I seek You for instructions on how to love (spouse's name) the way that You desire me to love her/him. I depend on the Holy Spirit to bring back to my remembrance all the things You have taught me and to lead and guide me into all truth. I praise your name always, in your son Jesus' name, Amen.

Day Eleven

Sow the Seed of...
Living and Loving in the Spirit

True love is a giving of love. Just as God is love, He is a giving God. He has proven His love for us by giving us Himself as shown in Genesis 2:7. He breathed His breath of life into us. In John 3:16, He gave His only begotten Son to save us from total damnation, and the list goes on.

Loving in the Spirit, put simply, is a renewed way of thinking and loving. It's God's way. God's love does not seek to receive but seeks to give, even when it appears that someone is loving or giving more than the other. Love is satisfied. Why? Love enjoys loving. Love is satisfied with and takes pleasure in giving; Love never tries to receive more than Love gives. True Love, a God kind of Love, seeks to give the advantage and never takes advantage.

Loving in the Spirit directly connects you with the Spirit within the person you love. There is nothing more pure than the God in you and loving the God in your spouse. You can see no wrong in another person if you are looking through the eyes of God into the eyes of God. The more you learn to love by the Spirit, the less control your flesh has over your thoughts, actions and emotions. This behavior gives you the God-designed marriage relationship that is filled with joy, peace, love, happiness and prosperity. Galatians 5:16 (NIV) says, *"So I say, live by the Spirit, and you will not gratify the desires of the sinful nature."* That means actions such as anger, fear, lust, distrust and untrustworthiness have no room to exist in your marriage. Think about how Jesus loves you and sow that same seed of love into your spouse. You are guaranteed a harvest of a love that makes you top priority over anything and anyone else. Your love will become one that is patient, kind, gentle, meek, longsuffering, good and most of all, never-ending.

Affirmation

Today, I commit to loving my spouse with the Spirit that God placed in me. I vow to only view the Spirit of God that lives in her/him. My life is filled with happiness, joy and peace because Love lives inside of me. God lives inside of me and I surrender ALL control of my emotions, actions and reactions over to Him.

Prayer

Father I thank You for the Holy Spirit that You placed in me to lead and guide me. Forgive me for not always depending on Your Word or the Holy Spirit. I know, according to Galatians 5:16, that if I commit my way of living to the Spirit, I will be able to resist the desires of my flesh. Father I declare that this Spirit rests upon me. He dwells in me and controls my every action. I thank You that my life is filled with a love for my spouse that is endless and only gets better, in Jesus' name, Amen.

Day Twelve

Sow the Seed of... Examining the Impact of Current Friends and Family

No one can ruin a marriage like friends and family. If you are not very careful, friends and family can become a negative influence to your marriage. In most cases, this influence appears as a sincere image of love and care. Friends give advice that appears to be helpful, but it can be the demise of your marriage.

Rules for Friendship and the Married Couple:

If he/she is not a friend of both the husband and wife, they have no place in your life, especially if they are of the opposite sex.

If this friend is not married, and/or non-spiritual, they have no advice to offer you concerning your relationship.

If intimate details of your sexual relationship are to be discussed, they must not be discussed with friends. This level of conversation should only be done with spiritual Christian counselors. Be aware that many cases of husbands/wives having affairs with their spouse's best friend are a result of visual images placed in their minds based on statements made by the spouse. You are the person who turned the friend on to your spouse! Watch your words.

Always seek spiritual counsel. Look for a couple who can serve as both counselor and mentor to your marriage. This couple must be a couple who not only knows the Word but also exemplifies it in their own lives.

Rule for Family Relations and the Married Couple:

Keep family out of your business. Although they may really mean well, it can sometimes be difficult for them to have an unbiased opinion. Gossip about your marriage can spread faster within the family and often faster than with friends. The only exception to this is if both the husband and wife agree that the family member is capable of providing wise, godly counsel.

This seed of examination will help you to identify two types of seed: 1) the seed that will produce the good fruit of healthy external relationships, and 2) the seed that appears to produce seemingly good fruit but eventually ruins even the good fruit. There was a song back in the 1970's that said, "One bad apple don't spoil the whole bunch." It was a great song, but oh so wrong. If you place one piece of rotten fruit in a bunch with good fruit, over time the bacteria from that bad piece will ruin even the good fruit. One negative, toxic, trouble-making friend or relative dressed as a loving, caring and concerned person can and will spoil your marriage, if you let them.

Affirmation

Today, I commit to conducting a close examination of those friends and family members who have some level of influence in my marriage. I commit to my spouse to disassociate myself with anyone who does not have the same godly character that I am in pursuit of. If my spouse and I are not in total agreement about who our friends should be, I agree to let them go at the cost of saving my marriage. My spouse IS my best friend and I depend on him/her along with the Holy Spirit for guidance and advice. I understand that loving in the Spirit requires an intimate relationship with God, which I commit to nourishing and cherishing daily.

Prayer

Father, I thank You for the people You have placed in my life. I pray that You would forgive me for not being a good steward over those relationships. I give You complete authority and rule over those who are in my inner circle. If there is anyone I am connected with who is not drawing my spouse and me closer to You, You have my permission to remove them from us. Your Word says in Proverbs 24:1 (Message), "Don't envy bad people; don't even want to be around them. All they think about is causing a disturbance; all they talk about is making trouble. It takes wisdom to build a house, and understanding to set it on a firm foundation...." Therefore, we should not keep company with anyone who will be a negative influence or hindrance to our marriage and destiny. I pray for discernment to know who is evil and who is of the Lord. It's in the mighty name of Jesus I pray, Amen.

Day Thirteen

Sow the Seed of… Constantly Discovering

We are fearfully and wonderfully made! God placed so much in us that we sometimes do not know all of who we are. Make it your daily mission to discover one thing in these three areas: Who God is, who you are and who your spouse is.

Seeking a better understanding of Who God is helps you to identify just how important a role He plays in EVERY aspect of your life. He is your source for life, health, happiness, wealth, peace, love, food, shelter... well, everything! Once you know and understand Who God is, your dependency and reliance on Him increases. That is exactly where God wants you to be. Total reliance on Him produces a content and worry free life that confesses, "All I need is HIM." This seed sown into your own life consistently will rapidly increase and bring a harvest filled with love, joy, peace and total fulfillment, all producing seeds that can be sown by you into the hearts of others.

Because of who you are—you might wonder sometimes what makes you click. We wonder why we respond to certain situations with fear or anger. We might wonder why we talk too much or too little; why we think the way we do; what drives us to make decisions, both wise and unwise. Many times our life experiences cause us to develop a pattern of thinking and acting that is so embedded in our minds that we think and act without realizing it. This type of behavior takes place in our subconscious mind. It's programmed in us and some reprogramming may be needed. At the close of every day, you should find yourself examining your attitude and behavior. Were you "Christ-like" today? Ask the Holy Spirit for a revelation of the things of which you may not be aware. Vow to change those things that have a negative impact on your life, marriage and relationship with God.

There is a lot to know about your spouse that can only be discovered in three ways: current situations/past experiences, conversations and a revelation from God. In some cases, conversations, situations and experiences can even teach your spouse something about themselves. Understanding your spouse is a never-ending course; however, it can lead to knowing better how to meet their needs and avoid those things that can cause animosity. This seed of constant discovery can produce a two-fold harvest: you learning more about yourself and about your spouse as well as your spouse discovering more about himself/herself and you.

Affirmation

Today, I commit to a continuous, never-ending pursuit of discovering God, my spouse and me. I believe that the information revealed to me, if used correctly, will lead to a life of increasing value, prosperity and enjoyment.

Prayer

By Your Spirit Lord, reveal unto me the things that You have prepared for me. Allow Your Spirit to search the heart of my spouse, for only Your Spirit knows the thoughts of man. I desire to know my spouse more and more that I might only bring good into her/his life. My heart's desire is to please You; therefore I seek Your wisdom, Your understanding, Your counsel, Your might and Your knowledge on how to please my spouse. I give You all glory and all praise, in Jesus' name, Amen.

Day Fourteen

Sow the Seed of… Learning the Essence of Forgiveness

"But if you do not forgive, neither will your Father in heaven forgive your trespasses" (Mark 11:26 NKJV).

Unforgiveness is rooted in fear. It is a very dangerous place to harbor in your walk with God and in your marriage. The key thing to remember is forgiveness is not about your spouse, it is about YOU! When you fail to forgive that issue, in most cases, the person attached to it now has control over you. They control your thoughts, your actions and your emotions; you are not at peace in the presence of the person or whenever that topic arises.

Forgiveness simply means letting go of the offense to the point that it does not have any impact on your thought life or your actions. Do not fool yourself into thinking that you have to forget about it; that is almost impossible. When you have forgiven a person, it no longer bothers you. Your reactions are as if the offense never happened.

Unforgiveness and fear are strongly attached. Not forgiving is a defense mechanism that we use to protect ourselves from being offended again. The problem with this is it does not work and it is not godly. Fear says, "I must protect myself." Fear is always about "me" and it is completely opposite of love. Love is not about me but it is about the other person. So to act in unforgiveness is to act in fear; to act in fear is a failure to love and a failure to love is a sin against God. As Mark 11:26 (NKJV) says, *"But if you do not forgive, neither will your Father in heaven forgive your trespasses."*

Affirmation

Today, I commit to fully understanding God's desire for forgiveness; this applies to me and others who may offend me. I realize that forgiveness brings about healing for me more so than for the person who offended me. Therefore, I must be quick to reconcile any offense, giving room only for God's love to grow. The sooner I forgive, the less time and room I give Satan to work at destroying my relationship and me. My relationship with God is most important, next is my spouse. I WILL NOT allow any offense to interfere with the growth of these relationships.

Prayer

Father, in the name of Jesus, I thank You that I am Your child. You loved me so much that You gave Your Son Jesus to die for my sins. Your Word says in 1 John 1:9 that if we confess our sins, You are both faithful and just and will forgive us our sins and cleanse us from all unrighteousness. I also realize that in order to receive Your forgiveness, I must forgive others who have offended me. I commit this day, according to John 20:23 to forgive the sins of those who have offended me and retain them no longer. Bring back to my remembrance anyone whom I may have offended. Then, grant me the opportunity to seek their forgiveness. I pray that the Fruit of the Spirit rest and rule over my marriage; the fruit of love, joy, peace, longsuffering, kindness, goodness, faithfulness, gentleness and self-control. They are all active in my life and in the life of my spouse and children. I praise You, honor You and glorify Your name, in Jesus' name, Amen.

Day Fifteen

Sow the Seed of… Speaking Words of Empowerment and Encouragement

"Let no corrupt word proceed out of your mouth, but what is good for necessary edification, that it may impart grace to the hearers." Ephesians 4:29 (NKJV)

Although difficult at times, always speak words of encouragement and empowerment to and about your spouse. We all know that words are not just a mere sound or a way of communication, but it was words that formed this world. The **Bible** says, "Death and life are in the power of the tongue" Proverbs 18:21(NKJV). Your constant complaining and ill-spoken words about your spouse can only be poisonous to your marriage. Likewise, positive and uplifting words can build your spouse up and eventually make her/him into the person who God desires her/him to be.

Never speak negatively about your spouse to anyone nor allow anyone to say anything negative to you about your spouse, even if it is true. By doing so you give them the freedom to always speak negative words about him/her. Sooner or later, when things are right between you and your spouse, you will resent the negative attitude and comments that you gave others permission to use.

As a husband, you can destroy your wife and create a woman of contention with your negative words, or you can empower her into the great woman God created her to be. Your wife looks to you for affirmation and encouragement. Proverbs 31 says her value far exceeds that of rubies and diamonds, for she is a precious gem. Verse 10 of the Amplified Version asks this question, "A capable, intelligent and virtuous woman, who is he that can find her?" The answer is YOU! Your wife is that woman. The woman of virtue is in your wife; it just may be covered up or masked by your evil and unkind words. Speaking to husbands about their wives, Ephesians 5:25-27 says in the Message Bible, "Husbands, go all out in your love for your wives, exactly as Christ did for the church - a love marked by giving, not getting. <u>Christ's love makes the church whole</u>. His words evoke her beauty. Everything he does and says is designed to bring the best out of her, dressing her in dazzling white silk, radiant with holiness." It's your Christ-like love that uncovers and unmasks the woman of virtue, the wife to whom you want to be married. Speak positive and affirming words that illuminate the beautiful gift from God that she is. You are making a queen for yourself so whatever you put in, expect to get that back multiplied.

Day Sixteen

Sow the Seed of... Understanding Marriage is TWO Individuals Trying to Live as One

God created humans as male and female. In this creation were all the characteristics of God because man was made in His image and likeness. He put Adam to sleep and made Eve from Adam's rib. It was at that point the characteristics of God that He placed in them began to form. He made some of His characteristics stronger in one over the other. For instance, His characteristic of desiring praise was placed in both man and woman, but made stronger in man. The characteristic of love, nurturing and caring was placed in both, yet made stronger in the woman. The two together acting as one presents the whole image of God.

Your life experiences, such as where you grew up; having lived in riches or poverty; and having lived with one parent, no parents or both parents helped to shape your personality. Other factors that may have contributed to your personality are: how you were treated as a child, your school experiences, your family and friend relationship experiences and any traumatic or emotional experiences. All these things helped to shape your worldview, which in time developed your personality. Your personality is the way you view life and how you respond to it; it is the way you see things and how you do things. Every person on this earth has a unique personality based on all of the circumstances discussed.

Attempting to blend the differences in individual personalities into one can be extremely difficult. Your human nature is to get the other person to change in order for things to blend well. This will never happen. This is much like placing two magnets together on the positive side or both on the negative side. Either way, they will repel each other and NEVER come together as one. However, if you take the positive side and match it up with the negative side, you cannot stop them from coming together and it is difficult to pull them apart. Once you understand that differences exist between two people and that this is simply how we are all made, you can begin to adjust your way of responding to them. If his/her electrons are spinning downward one day, yours need to spin upwards and vice versa.

We were made as one and we can live together as one. It is the small things within our individual personality that will attempt to attack your oneness. You should only plant seeds that are fruitful to your oneness. Things that attack your oneness are: selfishness, competition, a critical or criticizing spirit, unfaithfulness, and failure to obey God's Word. Placing the needs of your spouse ahead of your own and considering them in all that you do plants a seed of oneness that brings glory to God and His blessings upon you and your marriage.

Affirmation

Today, I commit to sowing seeds of oneness into my marriage. I vow to lose all selfishness and place the needs of my spouse ahead of my own. I commit to being the best possible spouse by not just meeting but exceeding her/his needs. I seek God for direction on creating oneness and destroying anything that may come against it.

Prayer

Father in the name of Jesus, I thank You for my spouse. I declare, according to Your Word, that we are one flesh. Our love for one another is a direct reflection of Your love for us; therefore, we are created in Your image and likeness. Ecclesiastes 4:9-12 says that a threefold cord is not easily broken; that includes You as the head of our lives, my spouse, and me. Psalm 133:1 (NKJV) says, "How good and how pleasant it is for brethren to dwell together in unity." I realize that there is power in godly unity and I desire to be the best possible person to express Your love for my spouse. Thank You for the unity of this marriage and the continual blessing of my family, in Jesus' name, Amen.

Day Seventeen

Sow the Seed of... Racing to Embrace and Say I Love You, Face to Face

When God formed man from the dust of the ground, He breathed the breath of life or the Spirit of life into a physical body. The desire for closeness and intimacy was already present as God made woman from the rib of man. Desiring to be sexually and nonsexually intimate, close to one another and touching affectionately is an inherent part of our creation.

Women desire nonsexual touching and affection because it says to them that they are important, desired, loved, cared for, cherished and secure. If the husband is only affectionate when his hormones are racing, the wife may feel like sex is desired more than she is. If sex does take place, it should begin with touching and affection long before and long after. As a husband, you might desire more than just the nonsexual touch. However, you must sow the seeds of a nonsexual expression of love including embracing, holding and cuddling. The more seeds you sow in this area, the more sexual your wife will become.

Contrary to what most women believe, men also desire touching and affection. This is an important need that is rarely met and often overlooked or taken for granted. While women enjoy public touching and affection, men, most of the time, prefer it privately. Touching and affection for men means something entirely different than it does for women. To men it means that the woman desires him in a sexual way. Although touching does not have to lead to sex, men enjoy being desired in a sexual way. Wives, your increased and consistent expression of sincere nonsexual affection will lead to increased sexual fulfillment by you and your husband.

Be eager and anxious to express love for your spouse. Always strive to be the first one who says, "I love you," and reach out to hug, hold her/his hand and kiss with no sexual expectations. This seed is a seed of love and care for the other person, not just what you receive. It is about what you give, and the more you give, the more you receive.

This affirmation should be done by both husband and wife simultaneously, if possible. This is about you doing what is right in spite of what your spouse is unwilling to do. Additionally, hugging, kissing and expressing your love and appreciation for your children are equally as valuable to the family. Your children, bearing witness to and being a part of this type of relationship, will be prepared to become healthy husbands and wives in the future.

Affirmation

Today, I commit to displaying love for my spouse by providing the type of touching and affection he/she desires from me. I vow to refrain from allowing this type of touching and affection to always lead to sexual activity. I know and understand that by me looking to satisfy a need in my spouse, I am providing a healthy balance of touching and affection combined with sex; therefore ultimately seeing my needs met.

Prayer

Father in the name of Jesus, I thank You for giving me a spouse who loves me and meets all of my needs. I thank You for giving me the gift of discernment to understand Ecclesiastes 3:5, the seasons and times to embrace and refrain from embracing and the times for expressing my love just by a simple touch. Thank You for Your love for me, for my spouse and most of all, for this marriage union, in Jesus' name, Amen.

Day Eighteen

Sow the Seed of…
Being a Partner and a Friend

Recognize that you are on the same side as your spouse. Many times we get into a tug of war in an attempt to control a situation or the marriage as a whole. Jesus said in Mark 3:25 (NKJV), "*If* a house is divided against itself, that house cannot stand." First, to prevent a definite failure during a disagreement, you might consider "agreeing to agree." Find some common ground that you both can stand on and build from there. Second, you must analyze the degree of your selfishness in the situation and get rid of all pride, as we know pride can only lead to contention. The enemy is not your husband; it is not your wife; but it is that thing that is causing division to surface between the two of you. GET RID OF IT!

Commit to being a friend to your spouse. Be one that she/he can trust with intimate details about their lives. Be the person who is in the struggle with her/him, not just another person watching from a distance. Be the one who sympathizes when sympathy is needed and a motivator when encouragement is needed. Be likeable. Be your spouse's partner. Be the one who is on the same team with the same goal in mind. Be an active part of her/his everyday world. Be <u>knowledgeable</u> about their life at work, home, church and in their social circle. Be an ear, not a mouth!

How can you sow the seed of friendship into your spouse? Provide them with self-initiated, heart-felt sincere encouragement at times when your spouse needs it most. Do not wait for your spouse to hint around or to tell you he/she needs it, just do it! Be in touch with the things that are going on in her/his life and always be prepared to do something to make her/his day better. Do not always call with a problem or a serious conversation, just be silly, have fun. Be the part of his/her world and the place they can run to and find joy! The harvest from this seed is plentiful. Being a friend means there is a second party involved; the more you pour into your friend, the more your friend will pour back into you. When this friend is your spouse, you can't get any better than that!

Affirmation

Today, I commit to being both a partner and a friend to my spouse. I realize that I'm married to her/him because of the love and joy she/he brings me. I chose this person to be my spouse and I am totally committed to bringing her/him happiness, love, joy and contentment. I thank God for my spouse daily and when a disagreement occurs, I recognize that it is not the person that is causing the division but the issue itself. My spouse is my teammate and we are pursuing the same goals and dreams. It is my personal goal to be a better friend to my spouse than she/he is to me.

Prayer

Father I thank You for my spouse, my lover, and friend (name). My spouse is truly a gift from You and I desire to be a better friend to her/him than she/he is to me. I know that God loves us dearly because He has given us the Holy Spirit to fill our hearts with His love. We desire to always love one another and work together with one heart and one purpose. Grant me wisdom, O Lord, and insight that I might always walk pleasing in Your sight and in the presence of my spouse. I desire to be the perfect complement to my spouse. Thank You for hearing and answering my prayer, in Jesus' name, Amen.

Day Nineteen

Sow the Seed of… Understanding, Everybody Plays the Fool Sometimes!

The book of Proverbs deals with the fool quite a few times. Why? Because everybody plays the fool sometimes, yes, even you. It is important to understand that it does happen. It is also important to recognize when the fool is present and how to respond to the fool. Proverbs 4:23 (NKJV) tells us *"to guard your hearts with all diligence."* Why? *"for out of it flows the issues of life."* When we fail to guard our hearts (mind, will and emotions), we tend to take on the role of "the fool." Acting a fool will lead to a very damaging behavior and if that attitude is not regulated, it can snowball into a very unhealthy marriage. Check out what Proverbs in the Message Bible says about the fool.

Proverbs 12:15-16
"Fools are headstrong and do what they like; wise people take advice. Fools have short fuses and explode all too quickly; the prudent quietly shrug off insults."

Proverbs 18:2

"Fools care nothing for thoughtful discourse; all they do is run off at the mouth."

Proverbs 23:9

"Don't bother talking sense to fools; they'll only poke fun at your words."

Proverbs 26:4-5

"Don't respond to the stupidity of a fool; you'll only look foolish yourself. Answer a fool in simple terms so he doesn't get a swelled head.'

Proverbs 26:11

"As a dog eats its own vomit, so fools recycle silliness."

Proverbs 28:26

"If you think you know it all, you're a fool for sure; real survivors learn wisdom from others."

Proverbs 29:11

"A fool lets it all hang out; a sage quietly mulls it over."

Playing the role of a fool is a seed you do not want to plant! Why? The harvest is so, so plentiful. When you get two fools together, it's like sowing a seed, then watering it with steroids! The seed you want to sow is one of wisdom, and this one is so easy to sow because God will freely give you wisdom in every situation you find yourself. Always be wise in your speech, actions, thoughts and your responses. A soft response can diffuse anger and wrath, but harsh, mean and grievous words will only stir up anger and contention. *"Don't turn your back on wisdom, for she will protect you. Love her, and she will guard you"* Proverbs 4:6 (NLT).

Affirmation

Today, I commit to destroying the fool by displaying the character of Christ at all times. Should "the fool" show up in me, I will invoke Proverbs 4:23 by guarding my heart. I vow to be careful of my words, emotions and actions. If the other person is acting in the capacity of "the fool," I will invoke Proverbs 26: 4-5 by not arguing with a fool, lest there be two fools present. The fool does not think or act rationally, so I will strategically wait for a period of calmness and rational thinking to complete a discussion or get my point across. I realize that everybody plays the fool. It is nothing personal, nor does it mean I am less than a man/woman, but I quickly repent and reestablish my Christ-like behavior.

Prayer

Father God, I thank You for Your Word and I pray that You will forgive me for the times I failed to bring glory to Your name, and for the times I played the role of a fool in my life and in my marriage. Father, Your Word says in James 1 that "if any man lacks wisdom, let him ask and you will give it freely." Give me wisdom to handle all situations in a manner that pleases You. When Your wisdom enters my heart, I will be filled with knowledge and joy. I make my request known with thanksgiving, in Jesus' name, Amen.

Day Twenty

Sow the Seed of... Practicing Honesty Even if it Hurts

An open and honest relationship increases the level of love and intimacy in a marriage. Many times when we are faced with being truthful about a situation that is guaranteed to bring about pain and discomfort, we choose to lie or completely omit the whole truth. Although it is difficult for us to see, the truth brings about healing quicker than lies or looking for the right time to be honest. Eventually, the truth will find you out and when it does, the consequences are much greater than if you had confessed it from the beginning.

Our carnal way of thinking says the truth makes you vulnerable and gives complete control of the relationship and the situation over to the person you have offended; this is not entirely true. Dealing in truth gives God the control, so you must depend on Him for the outcome. When we depend on Him, He will cause all things to work out for good.

Ephesians 4:15 (NKJV)

"...but, speaking the truth in love, may grow up in all things into Him who is the head—Christ."

Ephesians 4:22-27 (NKJV)

"...that you put off, concerning your former conduct, the old man which grows corrupt according to the deceitful lusts, and be renewed in the spirit of your mind, and that you put on the new man which was created according to God, in true righteousness and holiness. Therefore, putting away lying; let each one of you speak truth with his neighbor, for we are members of one another. Be angry, and do not sin: do not let the sun go down on your wrath, nor give place to the devil."

Dishonesty is a clear indication of one's lack of reverence for the Lord and displays a lack of spiritual maturity. Speaking the truth helps us to grow up and mature in all things into Christ. Dishonesty has no room in our lives and especially in our marriages. Ephesians 4:25-26 says it is okay to be angry, just don't allow that anger to cause you to sin. Lying is a sin! Quickly, calmly and humbly seek to forgive yourself and your spouse, then come together to resolve the matter peaceably. The longer you wait, the more anger you allow to build and the more room you give to the devil to cause division between you and your spouse.

This seed of honesty is also a two-fold seed:

1) We should create a relationship with our spouse that gives him/her the freedom and comfort of knowing that his/her honesty will not be met with wrath. If your spouse fears telling you the truth, he/she is less likely to be truthful with you. You

should be slow to anger, slow to speak but quick to hear, quick to forgive, and quick to reconcile.

2) We should sow the seed of honesty by always speaking truthfully and dealing in truth, not just with our spouse but in all of our relationships. This seed of honesty paves the way for your spouse to accept, deal with and move forward beyond what may have gone wrong. The more truthful and honest you are with her/him, the better environment you build for your spouse to respond peaceably.

Affirmation

Today, I commit to total honesty in my marriage and in my life. I recognize that it is total honesty that brings forth emotional intimacy. Being honest with my spouse and others will strengthen my faith in God and the love my spouse has for me. I also commit to creating a peaceful and trusting environment where my spouse can talk to me without fear of anger or wrath.

Prayer

Father God, I thank You for Your Word. It is a light in my time of darkness; it brightens my pathway that I might be led into righteousness. My heart's desire is to put away all lying and evil speaking and to grow more Christ-like in all things. I am a woman/man of peace and seek peaceful resolutions quickly, that I might glorify Your name. I put away the old man and put on the new man which is created according to God in true righteousness and holiness. I depend on You and the Holy Spirit to lead me into all truth, therefore, freeing me from the law of sin and death, in Jesus' name, Amen.

Day Twenty-One

Sow the Seed of…
Knowing Right vs. Righteous

This is a seed that is sown directly into the heart of God and He is responsible for the harvest directly. What is righteousness? It is joy and peace in the Holy Ghost. Examine your attitude and actions against the Fruit of the Spirit which is: love, joy, peace, longsuffering, gentleness, goodness, faith, meekness and temperance.

Couples often find themselves in a tug of war over simple and sometimes senseless issues. Who is right? Who is wrong? With each person pleading his/her case, the tone of voice gets louder and firmer, sometimes even bringing in others to act as a juror. No one is willing to back down. Finally, a verdict is reached and the court rules in favor of evil, separation and divorce!

Anytime there is strife between a couple and no one is willing to compromise, they both lose. Being "Right" is not always the same as being "Righteous." You can have all the facts lined up, evidence and eye-witnesses, but if there is no peace and no agreement, then both suffer a loss. The "Righteousness of God" seeks to promote peace and well-being in our relationships. Being right only means someone else is wrong. As one flesh, there is no such thing as one being right and one being wrong.

WWJD?

Well, let's see, What Would Jesus Do? In John 8: 2-7, the Pharisees brought a woman to Jesus who was caught in the act of adultery. They wanted her stoned to death which was "right" according to the law. Jesus, acting in the "Righteousness of God," sought a peaceful resolution. "Let he who is without sin cast the first stone." According to what was "right" all would have been stoned; instead, "Righteousness" allowed the Pharisees and the woman to walk away.

A Command for Righteousness

Matthew 5:23-26 tells us to go to the person who has something against us and be reconciled. Notice the command is not on the person with the problem but it is on you to go to the person to reconcile the problem they have with you.

Imagine this: if you take the husband and put him in one end zone and the wife in the other, they are separated by one hundred yards of disagreements, some right and some wrong. In order for them to speak to each other without yelling, to embrace and agree, they will have to find common ground. This does not necessarily mean meeting at the fifty-yard line; one may have to walk seventy yards into the other's territory. One may even have to walk the full one hundred yards. The question is: Who is going to reflect the "Righteousness of God?" Someone should so that they can put an end to the division. When the enemy is given so much room, he widens the gap in that marital separation, and he will cause certain death to that marriage.

Affirmation

Today, I commit to living and loving my spouse with the Righteousness of God. Even if I know I am right, I vow to pursue peace, godliness and wholeness in my marriage. I WILL walk the full one hundred yards, even if my spouse does not take a step.

Prayer

Father, in the name of Jesus, forgive me for not walking in love, joy and peace, which is Your command for my life. I desire to dwell in a state of righteousness at all times, therefore pleasing You and bringing glory to Your name. I pray, O Lord, that Galatians 5:22-23 (the Fruit of the Spirit) is active and alive in me and not just during the peaceful times, but even when the pressures and challenges of life come. If there is strife between anyone else and me, I pray that You will grant me the opportunity to seek his/her forgiveness.

You Did It!

Congratulations on completing the 21 Days! My prayer is that you will continue to plant seeds of love in your marriage. God assured me through His Word that He would bless your marriage.

Get serious about your relationship with God, your marriage and your family. God loves you and He will answer your prayers for a great marriage. Your part in this is easy, you simply plant the seed and He will make it grow.

In closing, remember it does not end here. Go back to "Sowing the Seed of Realizing God's Love for You." Begin sowing this seed and go through this process continually, without ceasing or taking a break. In due time, you will notice the 21 seeds become a natural part of your daily life. Before restarting the 21 seeds, the last chapter is one that God laid on my heart during a time of study and meditation. It is a powerful, powerful piece that will bless you tremendously. It is entitled, "My Husband/My Shepherd." It is a parallel of one of the most well known Psalms in the Bible, the 23rd Psalm. Who needs to read this? If you are a husband or potential husband, this is what you need to strive for. If you are a wife desiring your husband to be this kind of man, here is some great news for you too. Make the virtuous woman in Proverbs 31 your role model for being a wife. Also, dedicate yourself to sowing these 21 seeds and to a lifestyle of prayer, then faithfully watch God transform your husband.

My Husband – My Shepherd

A Parallel of Psalm 23

Psalm 23:1-2 (NKJV) *"The Lord is my Shepherd, I shall not want. He makes me to lie down in green pastures; He leads me besides the still waters."*

In this passage, David is expressing his trust in the Lord as his Shepherd. He joyfully states his faith in the Lord as one who provides the best for him, leaving him wanting for nothing. He goes on to say that his Lord not only provides for him but He also provides the best by leading him to <u>green</u> pastures. These green pastures describe a place of prosperity and of needs being fulfilled. David describes his Lord as one who seeks peace and leads him in a peaceful way.

In parallel, this is the type of husband that a wife should be describing. He should be one who can be trusted and one in whom she can have faith. Her shepherd/husband is one who is providing only the best for her, leaving her wanting for nothing. His leadership is one of godly character, which is a peace that is equal to that of still waters.

Psalm 23:3 (NKJV) *"He restores my soul. He leads me in the path of righteousness for His name's sake."*

Here, David is saying that in his times of weariness or distress, his Lord refreshes and revives him, making him feel secure and safe. The Lord's leading is _in_ a pathway of righteousness, which means He chose to operate _in_ a righteous way first before leading His sheep. Righteousness speaks of one who neither seeks to be right or prove the other wrong but to promote peace. This righteous leading and restoration of David's soul is done for the namesake of the Lord, or better stated, to bring glory to the Lord. "For His namesake" simply means that the Lord takes pleasure in the prosperity of His people.

Husbands likewise should provide restoration to the souls of their wives. In many cases, the wife is working a full-time job, taking care of the kids and juggling many different responsibilities related to the family. Just the simple cares of life can be very demanding and stressful to her. As her lord, instead of coming in daily and dumping all of his stresses and work related issues on her, he is to provide her a place of refuge. He can restore and refresh her by allowing her to vent. He should share in or even take on some household and family duties. Also, he can take the initiative to cook, clean, set up a bubble bath for her (not with sexual intent) and make her comfort a priority. Since Ephesians 5:22 tells her to submit to her husband as unto the Lord, her husband, as lord, should take great pleasure in her prosperity for his namesake. Proverbs 31 describes a wife of noble character and it mentions in verse 23 that her husband has a good name for himself and is well known in the city. One reason for this is because the attention, care, and righteous leading of her husband has become evident in her, therefore he (the husband) is now being presented a glorious wife, without spot, wrinkle or any such thing (Ephesians 5:27).

Psalm 23:4 (NKJV) *"Yea, thou I walk through the valley of the shadow of death, I will fear no evil; for You are with me; Your rod and Your staff, they comfort me."*

Here we find David expressing his safety and security in the Lord his Shepherd. He says even in those times when he finds himself in potentially dangerous or threatening situations and times of darkness that seem to overtake him, he will have no fear. Even in the midst of "perilous times," David finds rest and security in knowing that God is with him.

David also says the Lord's rod and staff provide additional comfort for him. Just the mere presence of the Lord provides him with comfort. Why does David say he finds comfort in the rod and the staff? The shepherd's rod was used as a rod of correction. We often view this correction as a painful event. However, in this case, the shepherd used his rod to gently nudge the sheep when they were going astray or headed in the wrong direction. A prodding or nudging of the rod could be uncomfortable but its purpose was not to inflict pain; it was to impose enough *loving discomfort* to get their attention and redirection. Even if the rod caused pain, David viewed it not as pain but as comfort because it saved him from certain dangers.

The staff is a symbol of authority and power. Only the shepherd carried the staff and used it for various reasons. Primarily, it was used as a support tool to brace himself while walking on rough terrain. Throughout the Old Testament, we see the staff being used as an instrument to perform miracles. God placed a staff in the hand of Moses before sending him before Pharaoh.

So how does this apply to being a husband? Well, as lord or shepherd to the wife, she should find comfort and security in knowing that her husband is there for her and with her. She fears no evil even though there are times of darkness in her life and in the life of the family. His mere presence should be a safe haven for all of her discomforts; his presence should bring her joy. The husband's rod and staff are used in the same way as the shepherd's rod and staff. *"Your rod and Your staff"* are combined into one spiritual instrument and that is the Word of God. The staff (the Word of God), is not just a symbol of power and authority in the husband, it actually gives him power by way of the Holy Ghost. The wife should see the Word in him and it should bring her comfort. She should see the Word living and breathing on the inside of her husband. It is that same Word that he uses as a rod of correction, not for the purpose of beating her with it but for a loving correction. Whenever the rod is used, she may experience pain, just as the old saying goes, "The truth hurts." She should find comfort in knowing that it is because of his love for her that correction comes. In order for the husband to correct her with the Word, he must first know the Word. This "know" is not just knowledge of the Word but it is having an intimate relationship with the Word. The Lord that David spoke of was the Word, and as the lord of the wife, the husband should aspire to be the Word as well.

Psalm 23:5 (NKJV) *"You prepare a table before me in the presence of my enemies. You anoint my head with oil; my cup overflows."*

David moves now into a more evidentiary statement or proof of what he originally stated in verse one, "I shall not want." The evidence is feasting or celebrating in the face of trouble to the point of overflow. The word "table" is representative of a feast and David says here that this feast was provided for him in the very presence of those things that may come against him. What comfort there is in being able to feast on all that God has provided for you (both needs and wants), while having the ability to look directly at the things that are trying to destroy you.

David goes on to say, "You anoint my head with oil." This custom of pouring oil on the head was an expression of abundance and prosperity. In fact, it represents divine favor, prosperity and joy. David says not only do You anoint my head with oil but also, "my cup overflows." This overflowing is a symbol of overabundance.

As husbands, there should be some proof of provision and protection for the wife. She should be feasting on her husband's love for her in the very presence of those who mock and ridicule her for the prosperity he has provided for her. All of her physical and emotional needs are being met and she is getting so much love from him that it overflows. Since she has so much love that it overflows, there is no room for despair or for some smooth-talking man to get her attention. She knows nobody can love her and provide for her the way her husband does.

Psalm 23:5 (NKJV) *"Surely goodness and mercy shall follow me all the days of my life. And I will dwell in the house of the Lord, FOREVER."*

All that is good and merciful will be in pursuit of David. Contrary to any feelings of despair or discomfort, David says without question SURELY goodness will be behind me and something good will happen to me every day of my life." Even in those times when David was wrong or doing wrong, mercy was there to give him comfort and the reassurance of the Lord's love even though he did not deserve it.

David closes this Psalm with a decision. He says, "I will dwell in the house of the Lord forever." With all that love, peace, joy, prosperity, provision, protection, grace and mercy, why would he go anywhere else? He is going to stay right there!

Like David, a wife should see the goodness and mercy of her husband in constant pursuit of her. She should be sure of her husband's willingness and ability to provide for her, protect her and comfort her. Instead of greeting her with harsh words, demands or requests, he should seek to serve her. If she fails, disappoints or even angers her husband, his mercy as her lord should always be present. She should know that she can tell him anything: all of her shortcomings, mistakes and poor judgments and they will be greeted by his tender love and mercy.

As with the shepherd leading the sheep, the husband's rod of correction should bring comfort and his leading should be in the way of righteousness, which is to promote peace. His wife should be celebrated and honored by him giving her the desires of her heart; she should know that she is a *priority* and is *the priority* in his life. Her cup should be running over with his love and compassion for her every day! When he gives her "the look," that look should be one that communicates adoration, not retribution. His verbal and nonverbal communication should always say, "I adore you, you are beautiful, you mean the world to me, I will do anything for you." Even when she disappoints him, he should avoid communicating frustration, disgust, and most importantly, his superiority. Simply put, he should love her, not frighten her.

Everything in Psalm 23 represents love in motion. It is the active expression of the love described in 1 Corinthians 13:4-8. Likewise, when Ephesians 5:22 (NIV) says, "Wives, submit to your husbands as to the Lord," this Psalm is an example of "the Lord" the Apostle Paul was speaking of. Therefore, a husband should strive to be this kind of lord described by Paul, and his wife's response will be the same as David's response when he closes Psalm 23. She will choose to dwell in her husband's heart forever. She will endeavor to be a woman of virtue, one who respects and honors her husband. She will desire to live with him forever! He who finds this kind of wife finds a good thing, and the man who becomes a Psalm 23 husband will realize that he is already married to her.

ABOUT THE AUTHOR

After a successful tour in the Marine Corps, Winston spent the next 15 years climbing the corporate ladder working for several Fortune 500 companies. With seemingly everything a man could possibly want: family, great job, being a restaurant owner, and being a church leader, one thing was missing: a true understanding of God's design of marriage. After 21 years of marriage, it all came to a halt. Marriage, house, cars, job, and business all disappeared like a vapor. "With $40 to my name, a borrowed car, no job and living with my mother at age 46, God began to rebuild me." God has given Winston wisdom, knowledge, and understanding on the subject of marriage. He has been blessed with a new life, new wife, and most of all a passion for others who are struggling in their marriages. He is a mentor to several young couples, as well as single men and women desiring to be married.

In 2011, Winston published his first book entitled, "Marriage – 21 years of Doing it Wrong, 21 Days to Make it Right." This powerful 21 day devotional was written using the concept of sowing seeds of love into your marriage and allowing God to produce the harvest. Winston has been a guest speaker at several churches within the Florida/Georgia area. He has appeared on Pure Radio's "Terry & Terry Show" as well as on TCT's "Athletes with Purpose Show" with former NFL player Frank Murphy.

In December 2013, Winston released his second book entitled, "Preparing to Date Your Soul Mate." This book targets singles who desire to one day marry the person that God has for them. It's a thought-provoking look into the preparation it takes to be the best possible mate that God has to offer another. The book takes you through various stages of relationships such as falling in love with Jesus, living single while waiting for your mate, and how to attract the person you really want to be with. It also provides insightful information on premarital counseling, establishing mentors, financial planning and an in-depth look and understanding of the wedding vows.

For more information about Winston, visit his website or contact him via Facebook or email:

Website: winstontjackson.com

FB: Winston T. Jackson, Sr.

Email: winstontjackson@yahoo.com

Book Order Form

"Renew your mind to God's Design"

To order copies of this book and other books by Winston Tyrone Jackson, Sr., indicate the number of copies you would like next to the title, provide your shipping address and contact information, enclose payment including shipping, and mail this form to:

Winston T. Jackson, Sr.
P.O. Box 442343
Jacksonville, FL 32222

- Preparing to Date Your Soul Mate @ $9.99 each _____
- Marriage: *21 Days of Doing it Wrong, 21 Days to Make it Right* @$9.99 each

_____

                        Shipping and Handling: <u>$5.00</u>
                        Total Enclosed: _____

Shipping Address:

Name: _____

Street: _____

City, State, Zip_____

Phone: _____

Email: _____

Notes

www.ingramcontent.com/pod-product-compliance
Lightning Source LLC
Chambersburg PA
CBHW072057290426
44110CB00014B/1719